THIS PROJECT WOULD NOT HAVE BEEN POSSIBLE without *Orion* magazine and its work exploring the world through art and science. Thank you especially to *Orion* editor Sumanth Prabhaker and art director Hans Teensma for encouraging experiments. Thank you as well to Frances Collin, Trustee UWO Rachel Carson, for the permission to publish Rachel Carson's script and for blessing my lightly abridged version and to David Thomas at Broad Reach Enterprises for access to the final script. I'm grateful to my editor, Susan Van Metre, for wondering what this book could become and for the fact that, with the help of art director Nancy Brennan, it did become something. Thanks also to: Scott Ogilvie, who photographed the artwork and tidied up the images; Simon Kogan, who offered scraps of material and wisdom; Dr. Adam Soule and NOAA Ocean Exploration for sharing deep-sea experiences and video footage of the deepest explorations (which I highly recommend watching on their website). And to Jay T. Scott, who joins me in this life of wonder and holds my hand when we walk so I can look up at the sky.

To Oscar Soule, who taught me natural history, and to Linden, who notices and wonders

The text is an abridgment of the script "Something about the Sky," written by Rachel Carson for *Omnibus* and kindly provided by Broad Reach Enterprises. A previous version appeared in *Orion* magazine 40, no. 1 (spring 2021), as "Head in the Clouds: Reading a Language of the Sky."

First edition 2024

Library of Congress Catalog Card Number 2023945063
ISBN 978-1-5362-2870-0

24 25 26 27 28 CCP 10 9 8 7 6 5 4 3 2

Printed in Shenzhen, Guangdong, China

This book was typeset in Bodoni Six.
The illustrations were created from washi paper painted with sumi ink and cut with a knife.
The artwork was then photographed.

Candlewick Studio
an imprint of Candlewick Press
99 Dover Street
Somerville, Massachusetts 02144

www.candlewickstudio.com

and faded and moved and swirled like clouds constantly changing shape and form. I painted sheet after sheet of paper. When there was a tall stack of paintings, I let the unique hues of each sheet inform the image, molding my sketches to the play of ink. The stack of paper was a stack of possibility and chance. With minimal drawing, I cut images *with* the paper, not just from it. The paper and I had conversations about what might happen.

I pulled Rachel Carson into these discussions. What would she want to see? What *did* she see? I read her letters to hear her voice in my head. I used photos from her seaside cabin; of her brooches; her writing desk, pen, and microscope; of her trying to work while caring for her mother, nieces, and nephew. I felt as though I was making the work with her. That it was a collaboration. I had a new friend in addition to the sky and trees and shore; there was Rachel.

And her words! Her words are so calm and clean and comforting. The sky through which we earthlings peer into the vastness of the universe—into the past of distant suns—can overwhelm us with infinity. Rachel's words offer assurances. The sky is grand. It is mysterious and powerful. And yet it is what provides us life and security. The sky holds us to this earth, this wonderful earth. That request for "something about the sky" caught Rachel's attention. It wasn't a task to write everything about the sky. This was no assignment of certitude, but of curious wondering. She wrote to a friend of her desire to help people have "a new look at clouds—to make people feel that they are seeing them for the first time."

"It is not half so important to *know* as to *feel*," she wrote in *The Sense of Wonder*. To feel instead of know. That is what I hope this book gives readers, a feeling that makes you look up at the sky and wonder. As I write this note, a late-August breeze begins to stir on the sun-warmed land. The tide creeps up the beach and wets the hot, salt-dusted rocks. The rocks heat the air and a wind stirs, sending ripples across the water. Above the bare summer mountains floats a high layer of cumulous clouds with an even higher wisp of cirrus vapor. But it is the wind, the softness of the breeze, and the smell of the sea that connect the lofty clouds to me here on this beach, this sky to you, this book to Rachel Carson and her voice. Wonder. Honor and protect. But begin with wonder.

Who was Rachel Carson? Read more about this brave poet of science in her classic works *Silent Spring* and *The Sea Around Us*. What are clouds? *The Cloudspotter's Guide* by Gavin Pretor-Pinney (New York: Perigee, 2006) and the Cloud Appreciation Society website (https: //cloudappreciationsociety.org/) are great resources. Visitors to the website can even share photos of amazing clouds they've seen. For more about cloud names, NOAA adds a fourth type of cloud, nimbus, made of the three types of clouds that Carson describes (https://www .noaa.gov/jetstream/clouds/four-core-types-of-clouds). The World Meteorological Organization classifies clouds even further into ten types (https://public.wmo.int/en/WorldMetDay2017 /classifying-clouds). Each cloud is unique. Names are ways that humans try to understand them.

A NOTE FROM THE ILLUSTRATOR

IN THE FALL OF 2020, WHEN MY DAYS HAD ONLY SKY AND TREES AND SHORE, *Orion* magazine sent me words by Rachel Carson to see if I would illustrate them. Without reading them, I replied yes.

Yes because Rachel Carson changed how we think about science and progress. In her classic work, *Silent Spring*, she exposed how human-made pesticides and other biocides poison the ecosystem. Her words helped ban dangerous chemicals and awaken an environmental movement that still works to protect the earth today. She was a scientist who wrote many important books full of beauty and wonder. She contributed to the well-being of this planet. It is an honor to help share her voice.

In 1956, the American educational television program *Omnibus* presented her with a project. A young viewer had submitted a request to see "something about the sky." Moved by the youthful wondering, Carson wrote a script, and the segment, "Something about the Sky," aired on March 11, 1956. *Orion* magazine sent me the excerpts available publicly from this long-forgotten project. The parts were mostly about clouds. But I sensed there was more to it, a "something" that could form into a book. I contacted Rachel Carson's estate, and they granted permission to illustrate and publish the script but did not have a full version of it in their files. My editor located a first draft of the script stored in the Yale Library and a final draft in the archives of Broad Reach Media, the current owners of *Omnibus*. Carson's full thoughts about the sky, long tucked away, would now become a book-shaped "something" to inspire cloud gazing and wonder.

Illustrating sky and clouds posed a challenge to me. How could I depict clouds in my usual method of cut paper? Clouds have no defined edges, and their shapes keep shifting, forming, and dissipating. I wanted softer tones than the black paper I usually work with. Late 2020 was a time of change, and there was no going out and shopping for materials. I had to use what I had: ink, paper from a long-ago trip to Japan, the camera on my phone, an eye to the sky, and time . . . time to just watch and draw clouds. Not knowing what would happen, I began. I painted the paper with sumi ink, letting the ink pool and fade, forming layers of washes marked by the texture of brushes. I experimented, messed up, and kept painting. The ink bled

We are learning to read the language of the sky.

The air ocean, like the sea, is full of mysteries.

It is the high-riding cirrus that first beholds the sunrise and that holds the light of sunset longest, reflecting back to the dark earth the splendor of a light no longer visible—the rose and gold, the wine and scarlet of the sun. Halos seen around the sun or moon are the icy crystals of a cirrus veil.

Cirrus

Most ethereal and fragile of all are the high-floating wisps of cirrus, drifting just under the stratosphere. If we could approach them closely in an airplane, we would find them glittering in iridescent splendor like the dust of diamonds. Up in these substratospheric vaults of sky, from which the earth looks like the sphere it is, there is a hard, bitter cold, far below zero, summer and winter. So the cirrus clouds are composed of minute crystals of ice—the merest speck of substance.

Often the pattern of cirrus clouds is enough to tell us that a jet stream is passing overhead. A vast river of air is shearing a passage through the clouds. It is the strongest of all winds.

The jet stream sweeps the high clouds into characteristic patterns— like an artist's representation of motion and speed.

Once above it, all the water molecules blossom, through condensation, into the fabric of the cloud.

Most cumulus clouds have straight-edged bases, as though evened off by the stroke of a cosmic knife. Below this line, the air column holds its water invisibly.

Cumulus

Most beautiful in the infinite variety of their shapes are the cumulus clouds. As the earth warms under the morning sun, it heats unevenly. Invisible columns of warm air begin to rise from a plowed field, a lake, a town—any area warmer than its surroundings.

The column of rising air contains invisible molecules of water vapor drawn from vegetation, evaporated by the surface of earth or water. Such warm air can hold quantities of water in the vapor state.

Rising, the warm air cools; at a certain point, it can no longer contain its water invisibly, and the white misty substance of a cloud is born.

Fog of a different sort forms
when warm sea air rolls
in across colder coastal
waters and over the land—
shutting down harbors,
grounding planes,
isolating ships at sea with
its soft swirling mists.
When the same sort of
vapor drifts at a thousand
feet or so, we call it
stratus—a layer cloud.

Compared with the high-
drifting cirrus wisps and
the soaring columns of
cumulus, stratus clouds are
duller earthlings—coarse-
textured clouds formed of
large water droplets.

What of the clouds themselves? Despite their infinite variety of form, any cloud belongs to one of three basic types: stratus, cumulus, and cirrus.

Stratus

Rolling, swirling along the floor of the air ocean are the lowest clouds of all—fog. For fog is nothing but a stratus cloud so near the earth that sometimes it touches it.

Fog may shut down quickly on a clear autumn night when the air over the land loses its heat by rapid evaporation into the open sky.

Such a fog is a shallow one. Though we earthbound mortals grope blindly through it, the tops of trees may clear it, and in the morning the sun quickly burns it away.

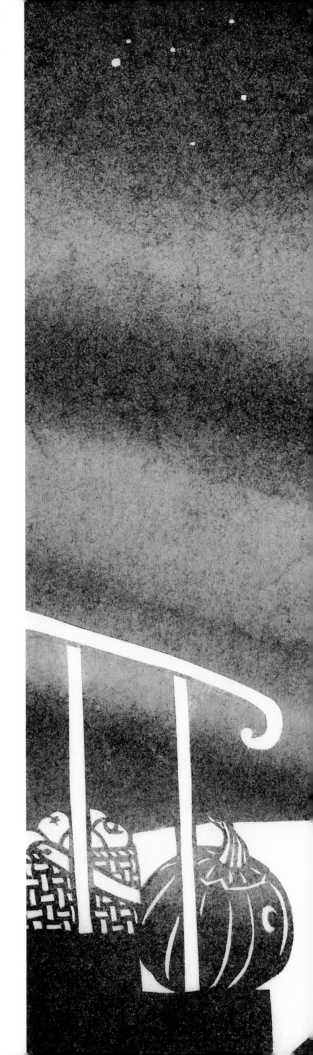

but often the cycle brings us nothing more troublesome than a gentle April rain— and always it is in the main a beneficent process, bringing the continents to life.

Sometimes the process
is marked by the violence
of storms. Sometimes
Nature indulges in the
wild fury of floods . . .

From the runoff of high ground—from melting snowfields and glaciers—the water finds its way to streams: noisy hill streams tumbling over rocky beds— the quietly rolling waters of valleys and plains—

all return at last to the sea.

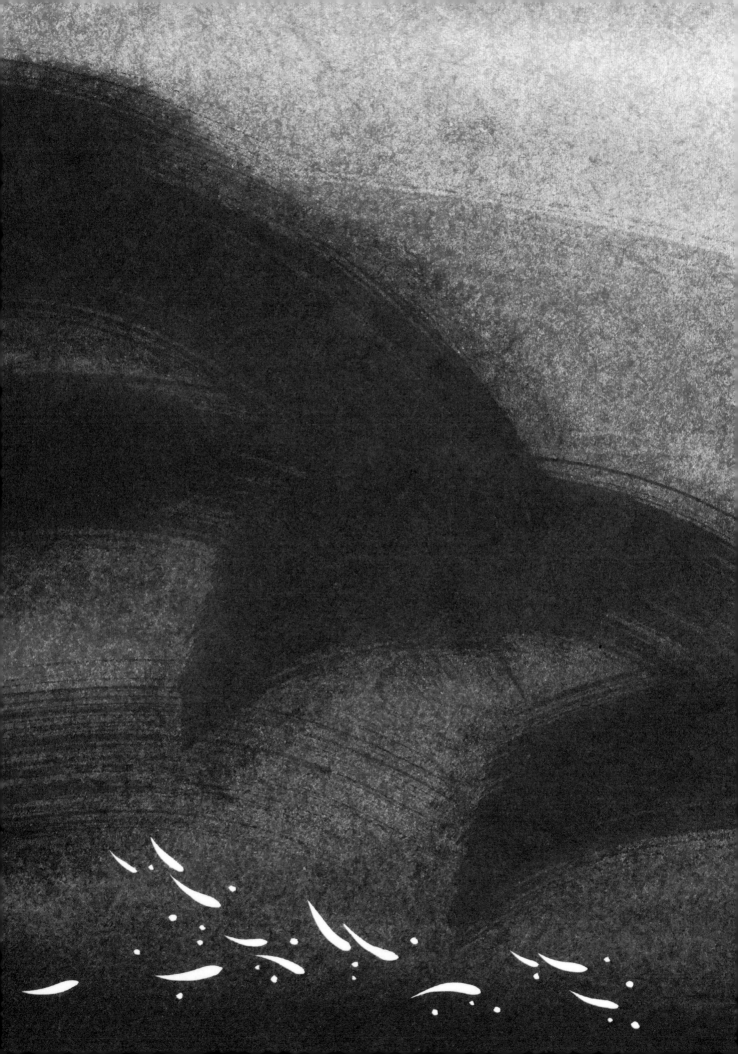

Or, in the cold regions, snow—a deep, soft, sound-absorbing blanket bringing a great quiet to the earth, storing moisture that will be released gradually to the thirsty land.

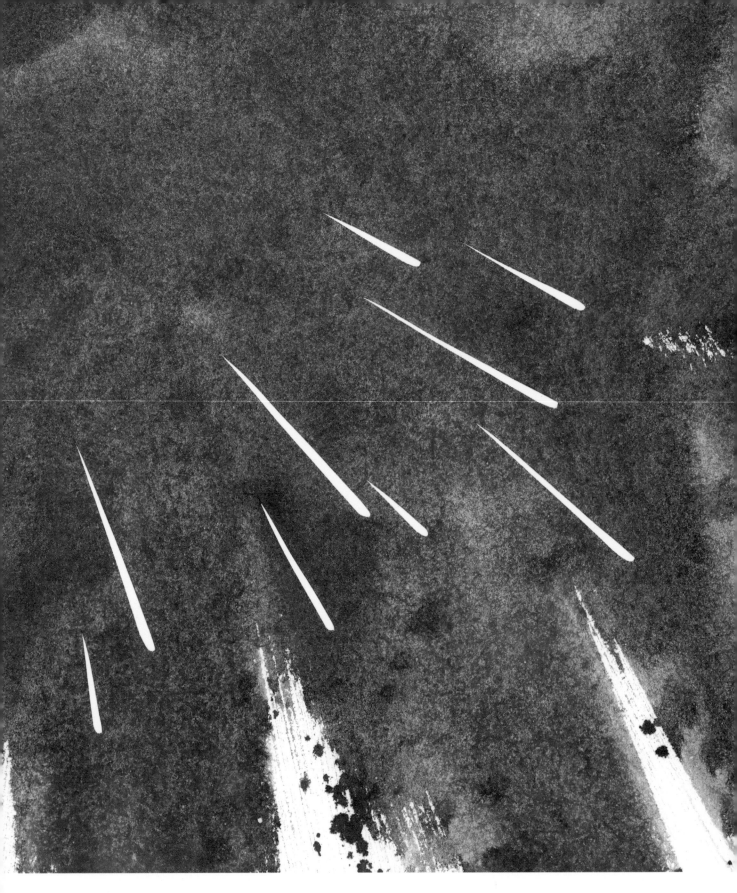

Rain falls on the earth—the end of a long journey that began in a tropical sea; yet in a constantly renewing cycle, there is no end, as there is no beginning.

Then, in a drama of turbulence and change hidden within the heart of the clouds, the water vapor begins to return to a liquid state—begins to drop earthward with increasing momentum.

Over all the vast surfaces of the ocean, stirred and broken by the wind, molecules of water vapor are escaping into the overlying air.

This occurs everywhere to some extent, but in the warm tropical seas on each side of the equator—the belt where the trade winds blow—the escape of water vapor into the air is tremendous. The warm, moist air rises; in the cooler air aloft, it condenses. Processions of woolly cumulous clouds are set adrift in the trade winds.

The moisture in these clouds may fall as rain and be recondensed several times, but it eventually becomes part of the vast circulation of the upper atmosphere—drifting over the continents—embodied in the clouds that day after day move from horizon to horizon.

Water from the sea is constantly being brought to the land. There, it makes possible the existence of plants and animals. There, in streams and rivers, it carves and molds the face of the land, cutting valleys, wearing away hills.

Without clouds, all water would remain forever in the sea, from which our early ancestors emerged more than 300 million years ago. Without clouds and rain, the continents would have remained barren and uninhabited, and perhaps life would never have evolved beyond the fishes.

Almost all of the earth's water is contained in the oceans that encircle the globe—all but a mere three percent. But to us inhabitants of the land, that three percent is vital. It is engaged in a never-ending cycle of exchange: from sea to air—from air to earth—from earth to sea.

Like the sea, the atmospheric ocean is a place of movement and turbulence, stirred by the movements of gigantic waves, torn by the swift passage of winds that are like ocean currents.

These movements of the air are made visible by the pattern of the clouds.

Look, for instance, at this ribbed pattern of high clouds. Like whitecaps on the crests of ocean waves, these clouds mark the crests of giant atmospheric waves— waves surging through space in an undulating pattern.

The bands of cloud mark the upsurges of condensation: the wave troughs of blue sky, the warmer air valleys of evaporation. Clouds give clues to the unseen structure of the ocean of air.

We, too, live on the floor of an ocean—the vast atmospheric sea that surrounds our planet. From airless space down to where it touches earth, its depth is some six hundred miles, but only in the lowermost layer, some six or seven miles deep, is the atmosphere dense enough to support life. Here, close to the earth in the zone of living things, clouds are born and die.

Our world has two oceans—an ocean of water and an ocean of air.
In the sea, the greatest depths lie about seven miles down. Life exists
everywhere. Corals—sponges—waving sea whips inhabit the bottom.
Fish glide through the sea, carrying lightly the weight of all the
overlying water. Waves move across it. Great currents flow through it
like rivers.

Clouds are as old as the earth itself—as much a part of our world as land or sea.

They are the writing of the wind on the sky.

They are the cosmic symbols of a process without which life itself could not exist on earth.

The farmer plowing his field reads the weather language of the sky. So does the fisherman at sea, and all others who live openly on the face of the earth.

For those of us who live in cities, awareness of clouds has perhaps grown dim. We may think of them only as a beautiful backdrop for a rural scene or an ominous reminder to carry an umbrella today.

of rain or snow.

storm clouds bringing portents

AMONG THE EARLIEST memories of each of us are the images of clouds drifting by overhead: fleecy, fair-weather clouds promising sunny skies . . .

SOMETHING ABOUT
THE SKY

CANDLEWICK STUDIO
an imprint of Candlewick Press

RACHEL CARSON
NIKKI McCLURE

SOMETHING ABOUT
THE SKY